WOULD YOU RATHER

GAME BOOK

WOULD YOU RATHER

own a toy shop or
an ice cream
parlor?

WOULD YOU RATHER

have grass for
hair or metal
teeth?

have a phobia
of carrots

or a terrible fear
of shoes?

WOULD YOU RATHER

be able to spit in rainbow colors or blow bubbles out of your nose?

WOULD YOU RATHER

own a zoo or a theme park?

WOULD YOU RATHER

WOULD YOU RATHER

crack a dozen eggs
on your head or
wear your shoes
filled with slime?

WOULD YOU RATHER

drive a tank or fly
a helicopter?

WOULD YOU RATHER

wear a toilet seat
around your neck

or a trash can lid
on your head?

WOULD YOU RATHER

be the size of an ant for a day or the size of an elephant for a night?

WOULD YOU RATHER

wear a frog costume to school or a clown outfit while walking around in the mall?

WOULD YOU RATHER

have a super long
tongue

or extremely
long fingers?

WOULD YOU RATHER

have a bed made
of chocolate or a
closet made of
cake?

WOULD YOU RATHER

swim in a pool of
custard or dance in
a pool of milk?

WOULD YOU RATHER

live in a circus
tent
CIRCUS

or a lighthouse?

WOULD YOU RATHER

have two birthdays
or two Christmas
celebrations every
year?

WOULD YOU RATHER

grow taller every
time you drink water
or shrink every time
you wear a hat?

ride a pig
in a shop

or a cow
in the park?

WOULD YOU RATHER

give up watching TV
or eating candy
forever?

WOULD YOU RATHER

be lost in a jungle or
in a sandy desert?

WOULD YOU RATHER

share your bed with a donkey

or a hippo?

have a bouncy castle in your garden or a slide in your house?

meet the Easter Bunny or Rudolph the Red?

WOULD YOU RATHER

wear a beard
of bees
or a hat
of rats?

WOULD YOU RATHER

be an angry rhinoceros or a grumpy penguin?

WOULD YOU RATHER

be able to sing like a blackbird or squeak like a mouse?

WOULD YOU RATHER

| WOULD YOU RATHER |

be a talking tree
or a walking
rock?

| WOULD YOU RATHER |

ride a bull or a
tiger?

WOULD YOU RATHER

be a bat

or a butterfly?

WOULD YOU RATHER

live in a house with no water or a house with no electricity?

WOULD YOU RATHER

have feet made of sponge or hands made of wood?

WOULD YOU RATHER

have a flying car

or a flying horse?

WOULD YOU RATHER

take a bath in your clothes or be wrapped up in toilet paper like an Egyptian mummy?

WOULD YOU RATHER

have a tame shark to go swimming with or a giraffe to walk to school with?

WOULD YOU RATHER

prefer
it rained
chocolates

or snowed
marshmallows?

WOULD YOU RATHER

give up your cell
phone or give up
your bedroom?

WOULD YOU RATHER

be able to see into
the future or unveil
all secrets of the
past?

WOULD YOU RATHER

have sharp
pointy teeth

or super long
fingernails?

WOULD YOU RATHER

wear your pajamas always or wear shoes that are a size too big at all times?

WOULD YOU RATHER

eat cake for breakfast every day or pizza for dinner every day?

WOULD YOU RATHER

wash your hair
with jam
JAM

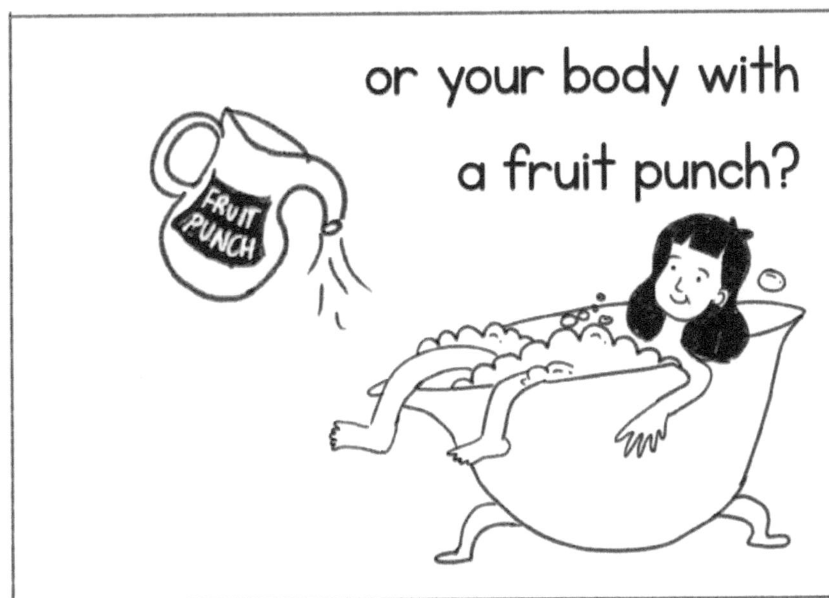

or your body with
a fruit punch?
FRUIT
PUNCH

be able to breathe underwater or be able to run for hundreds of miles without stopping?

have your skin turn blue or your hair turn green?

WOULD YOU RATHER

WOULD YOU RATHER

sneeze continuously
for an hour, or be
unable to stop dancing
for five hours?

WOULD YOU RATHER

have super-strength
or the ability to see
through solid walls?

WOULD YOU RATHER

WOULD YOU RATHER

walk for ten hours or hop for two hours?

WOULD YOU RATHER

build the world's biggest snowman or the world's most beautiful sandcastle?

WOULD YOU RATHER

WOULD YOU RATHER

live with a pack of
wolves, or alone on a
desert island?

WOULD YOU RATHER

meet an alien from
another planet or a
well-known pirate?

WOULD YOU RATHER

WOULD YOU RATHER

own a huge boat or a
small airplane?

WOULD YOU RATHER

be able to talk to
animals or be able to
read people's
minds?

have a dream about being in space

or a dream where you can fly?

| WOULD YOU RATHER |

be chased by
zombies or by
hungry vampires?

| WOULD YOU RATHER |

spend three hours on
a roller coaster or
bungee jump ten
times in a row?

WOULD YOU RATHER

live in a strawberry-shaped house

or a watermelon-shaped house?

WOULD YOU RATHER

take a tortoise for a walk or train a hamster to perform tricks?

WOULD YOU RATHER

dance like a chicken or bark like a dog when you wake up?

have tiger

or leopard

stripes

rosettes?

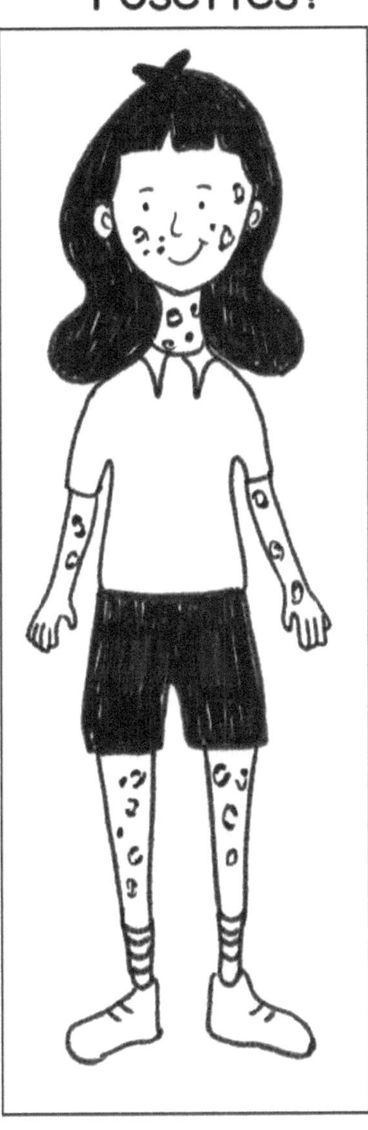

find a hidden treasure or a secret room in your house?

turn into a giant monkey or into a speechless little mermaid?

WOULD YOU RATHER

have a monkey's
tail

or a cat's
whiskers?

WOULD YOU RATHER

spend the winter in a
castle or the
summer in a
treehouse?

WOULD YOU RATHER

live in a cupboard
under the stairs or in
a haunted attic?

WOULD YOU RATHER
eat
onion-flavored
ice cream
ICE CREAM
ONION
FISH
MILK
or drink
fish-flavored
milk?

| WOULD YOU RATHER |

have a flying carpet taking you anywhere you want or a plate that provides you any food you want?

| WOULD YOU RATHER |

have the face of a baboon or the head of a hammerhead shark?

WOULD YOU RATHER

win an Olympic
medal

or an Oscar?

glow in the dark
when you hear music
or have ears that
play whatever song
you choose?

have your birthday
party on a boat or
play Easter egg hunt
on a steam train?

WOULD YOU RATHER

have legs
like a frog

or legs
like a chicken?

WOULD YOU RATHER

wobble like a jelly when you walk or make a bang like a fallen tree with every step you take?

WOULD YOU RATHER

have twelve toes on each foot or seven fingers on each hand?

WOULD YOU RATHER

never have to do
homework or be able
to go to bed whenever
you choose?

WOULD YOU RATHER

be able to type
incredibly fast or
read incredibly
fast?

WOULD YOU RATHER

never be able to stop smiling or never be able to stop winking?

WOULD YOU RATHER

give up shopping for a year or give up playing video games for a year?

WOULD YOU RATHER

WOULD YOU RATHER

have a pillow fight with your favorite pop star or play table games with your favorite actor?

WOULD YOU RATHER

be a character in a video game or feature in a cartoon?

have your neighbor's nose or your neighbor's teeth?

be a foot taller or a foot shorter?

WOULD YOU RATHER

be so heavy it's hard to lift your feet, or so light you sometimes float away in a breeze?

WOULD YOU RATHER

always wear a cape or always wear an eye patch?

WOULD YOU RATHER

WOULD YOU RATHER

have dinner with polar bears or breakfast with llamas?

WOULD YOU RATHER

smell of candy floss or orange blossom?

WOULD YOU RATHER

wear a clown's red nose or a clown's funny big shoes at the beach?

WOULD YOU RATHER

replace a President or a rock star for a week?

have a flower named after you or a street in your town named after you?

be famous for being entertaining or for being clever?

WOULD YOU RATHER

WOULD YOU RATHER

drink a milkshake on a roller coaster or share a sandwich with three drooling dogs?

WOULD YOU RATHER

be sat on by a panda or have a gorilla stand on your foot?

WOULD YOU RATHER

have an invisible friend who only you can see or know the answers to every question?

WOULD YOU RATHER

be on a reality TV show or have a book written about your life?

WOULD YOU RATHER

have to eat all your meals with chopsticks or drink every drink through a three-feet-long straw?

WOULD YOU RATHER

everything you touched was covered with ants or bees?

have to dig up your whole

garden with a spoon

or paint your entire house

with your toothbrush?

WOULD YOU RATHER

be able to jump as high as a skyscraper or be able to dive to the bottom of the ocean?

WOULD YOU RATHER

be able to turn mosquitos into ice cubes or falling leaves?

prefer a tree grew in the middle of your house or your house floated above the ground?

be able to control the weather or be able to turn into a cat?

WOULD YOU RATHER

own the world's largest rubber band ball, or the world's largest collection of umbrellas?

WOULD YOU RATHER

be able to make any object twice as big or make it change color?

WOULD YOU RATHER

WOULD YOU RATHER

have a job teaching
cats to sing or
teaching rats to
perform acrobatics?

WOULD YOU RATHER

have a nap on a
cloud or slide down
a rainbow?

eat an orange-flavored strawberry or a strawberry-flavored orange?

have Scissorhands or hammertoes?

WOULD YOU RATHER

be able to find anything you lose or never catch a cold?

WOULD YOU RATHER

be chased by bats or chased by bees?

WOULD YOU RATHER

have feathers
like a duck

or be furry
like a bear?

have a nightmare about being chased by clowns or a nightmare where you fall into a pit of snakes?

have a naughty monkey as a brother or a giant eagle as a sister?

WOULD YOU RATHER

wear perfume that smells of bacon or perfume that smells of grilled fish?

WOULD YOU RATHER

eat a sand sandwich or chocolate-coated mushrooms?

have an elf sitting on your shoulder or a fairy on top of your head?

watch a unicorn race or a dinosaur disco?

WOULD YOU RATHER

be captain
of a spaceship

or captain
of a pirate ship?

WOULD YOU RATHER

have a bedroom
that is always messy
or a bathroom that
is always messy?

WOULD YOU RATHER

have self-tying
shoelaces or a shirt
that never needs to
be washed?

WOULD YOU RATHER

find a squirrel in your school bag or a mouse in your coat pocket?

WOULD YOU RATHER

have a horse-sized dog or a dog-sized horse?

WOULD YOU RATHER

have a job as a scarecrow or a job as a mannequin in a store window?

WOULD YOU RATHER

be able to see in the dark or have a photographic memory?

WOULD YOU RATHER

| WOULD YOU RATHER |

wear a hat made of twigs or socks made of thistles?

| WOULD YOU RATHER |

prefer it was always snowing or always raining?

WOULD YOU RATHER

get locked in a library with a ghost or in a massive aquarium with a crocodile?

WOULD YOU RATHER

see a skateboarding penguin or a hula-hooping meerkat?

WOULD YOU RATHER

be made of metal like a robot or be soft and cuddly like a teddy bear?

WOULD YOU RATHER

play tennis with an apple or go bowling with a cabbage?

WOULD YOU RATHER

WOULD YOU RATHER

never be able to stop giggling or never be able to stop tapping your foot?

WOULD YOU RATHER

swap places with your teacher or with your best friend for a day?

WOULD YOU RATHER

prefer everything you
ate tasted of
pineapple or
everything you drank
tasted of tomato?

WOULD YOU RATHER

eat breakfast
standing on your
head or eat dinner
in the dark?

WOULD YOU RATHER

cure a dangerous disease or stop an asteroid from crashing into the planet?

WOULD YOU RATHER

eat a toothpaste pie or a soap pizza?

have a tree
growing
on the top
of your head

or strawberries
growing
between
your toes?

| WOULD YOU RATHER |

be able to juggle a dozen eggs or balance ten plates on your head while you do a jig?

| WOULD YOU RATHER |

be 100 years old for 100 years or seven years old for seven years?

WOULD YOU RATHER

have no reflection
when you look in a
mirror or no shadow
when you are out in
the sun?

WOULD YOU RATHER

be the world's
fastest eater or the
world's quickest
balloon burster?

WOULD YOU RATHER

be able to lick your elbow or be able to hum while you hold your nose?

WOULD YOU RATHER

have hair so long it touched the floor, or be totally bald?

WOULD YOU RATHER

live in a junkyard

or a fish pond?

| WOULD YOU RATHER |

cry tears of diamonds or find money in your ears every morning?

| WOULD YOU RATHER |

invent a time travel machine or a teleportation machine?

WOULD YOU RATHER

have to run a mile first thing every morning or brush your teeth for thirty minutes every day?

WOULD YOU RATHER

learn to ride a unicycle or teach a parrot to talk?

| WOULD YOU RATHER |

sit in an armchair
made out of bananas
or sleep in a bed made
out of pastry?

| WOULD YOU RATHER |

only ever wear red
or stripy clothes?

WOULD YOU RATHER

have giant
ears

or a giant
nose?

have the world's biggest slide or the world's biggest swing in your garden?

eat the hottest chili or the smelliest cheese?

have doughnuts for ankles or cupcakes for wrists?

have to eat all your food uncooked or all your food burnt?

WOULD YOU RATHER

lead a team of adventurers through the jungle or travel alone into outer space?

WOULD YOU RATHER

always have to wear gloves or always have to wear a helmet?

have a teapot
as your head

or the old buckets
for feet?

WOULD YOU RATHER

prefer a dog stole your ice cream, or a duck pecked your toe?

WOULD YOU RATHER

have a silly name or always have to wear a fake purple beard?

WOULD YOU RATHER

swim with sharks

or stroke a lion?

WOULD YOU RATHER

have a fruit-flavored carpet you could lick or a flashing wallpaper that turned your bedroom into a disco at night?

WOULD YOU RATHER

live in a hot air balloon high in the sky or in a deep cave underground?

WOULD YOU RATHER

grow a
sunflower
as tall as
your house

or pumpkin,
the size of a car?

WOULD YOU RATHER

all your floors were replaced with trampolines, or your kitchen turned into a swimming pool?

WOULD YOU RATHER

own a dragon or be a dragon for the weekend?

THE END

If you had fun while reading
this book,
please review it to encourage
the author.

With love,
Funny Lil Mommy